Unsafe

By Paula Telizyn

To Martin who doesn't care for poetry
and yet, somehow, was the inspiration
behind this book. Isn't life fun? :)

Honestly, this book is a bit
deranged coupled with a tinge of
madness.

I'm convinced it came out of playing
too much chess online and trying to
defend my standing.

Spoilers: my standing needed a
better defender. But on the upside,
you, Dear Reader, get this book. A
tiny consolation, perhaps best used
as a fire starter.

May all your fires be warm,
contained and blessed.

With love

Paula Telizyn

2021

Table of Contents

FALL

Noxious impressions
Flickering hopeful

I am a glittering tower
Very cold within the light
Smell my splintering inspirations
Unlearn my past

The clock demands
Claiming all the life you have
Don't wait!

Autonomy is an illusion,
A teasing poison,
Mist in the hand.
It was never there.

Opaque silence remains.

xiv

xiv

I met a girl
I fell in love
She was strange poison
A brilliant siren in my dream

I met a girl
I fell in love
She carried her darkening defiant
Broken heart

She took my luggage
and left her own

Live, laugh, love
A script for mundanity
Deny the pleasure
Tighten your wig!
The pleasure shall flee.

Live your best life,
Weep in the darkness.
Mask on, feathers present
Splintering over the shadows.

YOLO I say,
The fool gets weird.
Greying, hungry,
Crossing again and again.
All you need is a little motivation.

Swallow your hope,
Red lips pursed.
Wander aimlessly
Not knowing why.

I wish to be your comforter, but wait
Sit this feeling, down this mortal surrender.
Renew the music of that voice, that joy?
Leave the new song; release and say:
Back to the lost!
You shall not know gracious care
To crown your dear old head.

I feel lost tonight;
Darkness there with a stars' delight.
How should I hope, amid a ray,
The blackness of my very sky?
Filled with deep passion, this rude breath.
That in a dream of its own sleep,
A music of deep, untold rest.

Stop for a while,
While the snow falls,
Evil and peaceful on the light.
Melancholy has arrived,
Shadowed grieving.
Does anybody see it?
A dull sameness dogs its heels.
While the snow falls.

Despair weighs heavy,
I live to regret tomorrow.
The ground, a respite relinquishing no love.
I fade, even in the sun,
An untrustworthy memory.
Carry on.
Carry on.

xxvi

I'm lost and I'm all alone
I'm lost with nowhere to go
I'm lost and I'm lonely
I'm lost with nowhere to go

People
With their lives in their hands
And their heads empty.
Do they think of the things they could buy?

XXX

XXX

All of these people talking
With their advice in their bags.
A quiver, a tremor,
Fleeting and gone.

They think they're something
When they are nothing at all.

Grass never questions
It's green
It grows
It thrives
Or not
Be more like grass

Be afraid to be who you are
Go through life with regret
You're   still   you
Don't waste your time and grow

xxxvi

A desperation, however hard it tries,
Will always be suicidal.
Now self-destructive is just the thing,
Anguish is unsafe.

The emotion that is cruel,
Above all others: anxiety.
Are you twisted by its torturous embrace?
Feel it gasp and flail.

The fat agony sings an unendurable melody.

LAW

When I think of lambs,
I see a foetal development.
Never forget
the humorous
and
buffoonish
lambs.

x1

The stink is gone,
Sinful and grotesque within the air.
I feel heavy sirens near;
The insanity is fleeing.
Evil and brilliant rain:
It seduces invisible claws against the land.
The twilight shall flee
Greying awake,
Crossing the frontier
A ticking clock.

Dark and flying beside the earth
I smell green toads behind the trees
Take cover! The inspiration has died

Paula Telizyn is a writer, visual
artist and mentor living in Canada. She
has birthed numerous demon spawn, has
too many cats to count, and has now
lived her dream of being a a TV chef,
except it was online and only 27
people watched.

You can find her on Twitter and TikTok
at @PaulaTelizyn and on the web at
www.PaulaTelizyn.com

www.ingramcontent.com/pod-product-compliance
Lightning Source LLC
Chambersburg PA
CBHW051337150726
47997CB00004B/1504